I0145541

The Return of Sound

Poems

Zahava Sweet

Bombshelter Press / Los Angeles
2005

Copyright 2005 by Zahava Sweet

Grateful acknowledgement is made to the publications in which the following poems have previously appeared:

"The Line" in *Port Townsend Ledger*. "Dark Whispers" and "The Line" in *ERGO!*, Bumbershoot Literary Magazine. "Scarred Table" and "Black Moss" in *Semi-Dwarf* and "Ilan Ramon" in *Jewish Community News*. "The Treasure" in *ONTHEBUS*.

Cover, layout, and book design by Ron Sweet, Sweet Advertising & Design.

Author's Acknowledgements

I wish to thank my teachers, poets and friends for their support and faith: Peter Levitt for his incredible insight, Jane Hirshfield for being the teacher of my dreams, Ethna McKiernan for wonderful feedback and a keen ear, Phyllis Pivar who spent hours on the computer creating a preliminary manuscript.

A special thank you to Robert Bly for early inspiration and teaching.

A very special gratitude to Jack Grapes for his excellent focus, deep insight, and abundant energy in shaping the manuscript.

My many thanks to Ron Sweet, with love, for his teaching me the computer (which wasn't easy), for his time and expertise in designing and arranging this book, that without him would not have come to light.

Bombshelter Press
P.O. Box 481266
Bicentennial Station
Los Angeles, CA 90048
www.bombshelterpress.com

The sound, the voice returns to free a silent suffering. In tears or in a chuckle. The eternal flame—to keep the retrospection alive.

Blessed Morning

I wanted to write
one poem this morning,
just one little poem
but in that moment
a bird warbled
just once.
There was an echo
above the barking dogs
the trumpeting cars.

One little song
one musical note
as short
as the beat
of the heart.

Contents

To My Mother

Roots

The Mountain Ash outside
was born lucky.
It replenishes itself each spring,
waves its leaves in a new rhythm,
gulps the wind, drinks the rain.
It knows how to survive,
splendid with its roots
deep in the earth.

Trees don't yearn for faraway cities,
new homes. They remain
with old companions.
Winter comes, snow,
a storm knocks down branches,
yet the trunk remains sturdy,
supported by its nest of roots.

We humans wander
wars come and go
and misplace us.
We keep going
wandering
through strange countries
new cities.
We wonder where is
the next destination
a station in between trains.

Rogowska Street

Where is Rogowska Street
and my home?
In the grey courtyard
I played hopscotch with Mascha
and watched Kazio skip,
his knees bare
even when it snowed.
How I admired him
in his short pants,
how impervious he was to cold.

My home was there
on Rogowska Street
My mother, father, sister
were there,
a childhood enveloped
in white silk.

The tall grandfather clock
Father used to wind
with a silver key.
The blue Keren Kayemet box
we dropped coins into saying
next year B'Yirushalayim
in Jerusalem.

My mother's thick hair
wrapped around me
like a warm cape.
The Shabbat candles
she blessed
in a silver candelabra
on Friday nights.

Where is my home
in Brzeziny?
Where is my home
on Rogowska Street?
The Street my mother walked along
in a white blouse
holding my hand.

Do ghosts live there,
in our house
on Rogowska Street ?
Do they torment the living
with long fingers of memory?
All these piles of bones,
disintegrated.
No one knows where.
There are no graves to sit by.

Only their names
listed in crumbling books
some student will thumb through
in a library.

Mamusiu, Mother

In the black crown of your hair I hid
from Father's step.

I watched you say the blessing
over Shabbat candles,
your soft lips, your low voice.

Your face delicate in the light,
slender fingers fluttering over flames
like holy leaves.

Around the carved mahogany table
we gathered, its thick legs
and clawed feet like that of a lion.

On a white linen cloth
Shabbat candles burned,
a challah, a kiddush cup in festive light.

Even father was amiable on Erev Shabbat.
He put his kippah beside him,
ready to pop it on

the moment grandfather Eckstein
appeared to take his place
in his special chair.

I climbed into my grandfather's lap
and under the tall black hat
made little braids
of his silver beard.

In the golden challah
your face shined,
father's small hands crumbled food
on the white cloth.

This was a time before the beginning,
when your fingers fluttered over the flames,
when the light still flickered
in the ashes.

Father

Father was a wolf
in the forest.
He entered our home
in a storm,

his polished shoes mirrors
that clanged on the floor.
His voice penetrated the walls
a roar,
paintings trembled
within their frames.

The white linen cloth
flew to the ceiling like a cloud,
the asparagus plant sadly folded
its needles.

And I ran to hide
in Mother's black hair,
a thick unpenetrable
wall of love
tall, tall as heaven.

Dark Whispers

Grandmother
sorts potato peels in the sink
for our supper.
"My children gone," she sighs.
"The oldest and the youngest gone."
I hide in the black folds of her dress,
will my mother come back?

The light of day faded
in grandmother's house,
the room dark as her dress.
I sleep in the empty bed,
my mother's hair
in the blankets.
Her fragrance of konwalja. If I wait
the door might open.
She will appear in her seal coat,
her voice,
pearls of the sea.
Perhaps she'll come
through a window in the sky,
fly in on wings,
a raven or an angel.
Maybe I could take
a strand of her hair
to wear
on my finger.

The Return of Sounds

The rain falls all around me.
From my childhood piano
I hear the music, the old music:

My feet splash
in puddles of summer rain.
Mother plays water music
in a porcelain basin,
The great grandfather clock
chimes in a thundering basso,
two silver spoons drum
on the table top.

And I am sitting at the large piano,
my feet barely reaching the pedals.

I listen to
    rain music
    water music
    the basso
    the drum

and with trembling fingers on the keys,
I begin to make music too.

Winter's Grip

Once, on a cold
sunny day
the wind whispered
a melody in my ear.

It sang,
"On a day in spring
a bird gathers straw
to weave its nest

a daffodil opens
its yellow face

a caterpillar
gives birth
to a butterfly

on a day in spring
the wind hums melodies
of mating and love."

I noticed winter
still sitting
at my door

with icicles
for his beard
and a skate
in his hand.

"Krin, krin, krin"
he said. "Won't you
come skating
with me?"

"Well," I said,
"The wind told me
spring is here
but I can't see it.

If I go with you
I will not see
spring."

"Krin, krin, krin
You only hear
The wind's voice
tell you about spring,
but you can't see it.

If you come with me
you can play
and enjoy winter,
krin, krin, krin."

I looked down
at his white arm
and said, "I want
to wait for spring,

I want to see birds
lay eggs in their nests
I want to see buds
open into flowers

I want to wait
for spring."
And I stamped
my foot
in the hard snow.

With one sweep
of his white arm
winter held me tight
to his cold body

and on his skates
we slid down valleys,
up hills
and down again.

Trees looked stiff
with their
white branches
and the air
snipped at my face
like a knife.

We traveled
a long way
and when I looked up

the sun was high,
and when I looked down,
winter's beard
had become water

and out of his arm
I slipped
to the ground

there, a small patch
of soil peeked
from under the snow.

I put my cold hand
on that patch

and heard the wind
hum faintly
in my hair.

Straw Flowers

My mother used to keep them
on our commode. Colored as daffodils,
they were little suns shining.

Dolls on a blanket,
and my mother my playmate.
She entered my world
of fantasy and dreams.
A princess imprisoned
in a castle.
A troll lurking in the river.

At night I slept
in a white crib,
its sides netting,
a hammock.
Through the openings
I squeezed my nose and toes.

After cold nights
when the snow had fallen
I traced flowers
on morning windows.
My mother heated a blanket
on a furnace,
and put it on me
with her hands.

I nestled
down under the blanket
the sensation of her hands
still on my arms,
and curled inside her fragrance
as I fell
into the deep sleep
of childhood.

The Crib

The sides of the crib
were made of white netting.
I pressed my face
into the squares,
wriggled my toes
through the openings.

I could see my mother and father
in the room
talking

next to the tall
grandfather clock,
its etched flowers in the glass,
the golden pendulum
choosing the moon, the sun,
          the moon, the sun.

In the ghetto
my sister and I
slept in that same crib,

the netting torn
from our two bodies
pushing against each other
in that small space.

Elbow to elbow
head to head,
when one turned
the other awakened
in the small room
where everyone slept,
or pretended to.

Sometimes we faced each other,
Sometimes, back to back
our bodies always
pressed against each other
in that small room

where everyone slept
or pretended to
choosing the moon, the sun,
    the moon, the sun.

A Dream

I saw a golden braided challah
large as a five month baby.

I scooped the white bread
from inside,

slid my head
into the hollow crust
and smelled its aromas:
chocolate, bananas,
chicken soup
and matzo balls.

I was about to walk outside
with the challah on my head
when I heard a shriek —

"Verboten!"

I woke in the small bed
beside my sister
and saw the kitchen
still clean and bare.

A Purim Dress

Mother designed it, cut the satin
trimmed it with white fur.
I was the snow queen
on Purim night
the queen of white fields
of cheerful trees
in feathery branches,
of snow men in black hats
and carrot noses.
I was the queen of snowball fights
and sleigh rides.
At night, when Mother and Father
fell asleep,

I slipped on my white dress
and stood in front of the mirror
whispering poems to myself.

They penetrated the door
to my house, the soldiers
in gray uniforms armed with rifles.
Silk and linen spilled onto
the floor.
The Snow Queen gown
a white puddle. One held the dress
on his rifle. From under the bed
where I hid I heard him say

*"Das Kleid wird sein fur meine Tochter,
meine kleine Helga. This dress will be
for my daughter, my little Helga."*
He folded the dress gently
and stored it under his arm.

I dug my fingers into the floor.
My heart thumping in my chest.
Why didn't Father or Mother
do something ?
Why did they let him take my gown?
My white satin gown.

My Snow Queen Purim dress?
I saw their faces gray and folded
like elephant's hide.
Maybe they too became children
waiting for someone to protect them.

In my home, on Rogowska Street,
the pendulum stopped. The tall
grandfather clock fell silent.

The First Period in the Ghetto

You were gone
and no one was there
to tell me
what to expect.

I didn't understand
what those
stained sheets meant.
I was afraid
but I had to tell
Grandma.
She smacked my behind
briskly.
It didn't hurt,
but I was surprised.

Well, this must have been
the custom,
to greet such events.

Later she whispered
to my father
and he looked up
from his bowl
of watery soup.

I wished then
there was a hole
I could fall into.

You Vanished

to my Mother

I have memorized the color of your absence.
The cloth that never wrapped your body.
Your fingers climbing the walls
of an empty grave.
I want to know how you died.
I want to hear it from your lips
which left their imprints on my face.
I want your hair spread around me once more.
Perhaps it is the sea that claims you,
the fish nibbling at your hair.
Long strands of sea-weed
wrap your body, while corals
attach themselves to your belly. But no,
it was not the ocean that took you.

I don't know who did, or why.
You disappeared one snowy night.
You went down the stairs
from Grandma's house.
The frost gripped you. Dark arms.
You vanished,
not even your familiar scent
of konwalja remained.

They took you. They took your gold rings
and stole your black crown of hair.

I have an old photo of you
wrapped in a soft cloth.
How would you be today?
I see you – in the crown of your hair,
the satin of my white Purim dress,
Your voice whispers my name – *Zosienko*.
I am the girl in the snow queen gown
with hair like straw and serious eyes,
the child who would slip a hand into yours
to be led for miles.

I go to a place in the forest.
Where it is quiet among the trees.
Your hair wraps around me – a shawl.
You carry a basket of wild strawberries
small as tear drops. And you collect driblets of rain.
They shine on green leaves. You take a berry
between your fingers, from your hand to my mouth.
The taste of blood.

Black Moss

I see her hair,
a black wave,
the verdant sponge
of the forest.

In her arms
she held me,
her hair
above my heart.

She played dolls with me
on the wooden floor
of Grandma's home.

A grandfather clock
swung its pendulum
to the moon and sun
to the moon and sun.

1941. The pendulum stood still.

She walks down the stairs
of Grandma's home
her black fur coat
in her arms.

She opens the door
and walks out
into the pinching cold
closing the door behind her.

I open the door
she had just closed,
step out next to her
and hold her hand.

Branches of an oak
gripped by frost.
Two men snatch her away,
walk her to the curb,
squeeze her into a car
with gray windows.

I want to say a word
to yell,
but my voice
freezes in my throat.
My eyes are on her
footprints in the snow.

I turn back to the house,
walk to the front steps,
open the door
and return to
Grandmother's house.

Grandma's home is silent.
the table bare, the laughter gone,
the silver knives too
that blinked to the spoons.
Silent

as if black spiders
marked with blood
had crawled out of the walls.

No stone or pebble
mark her place in the earth
where I could bring
my flowers.

She must be somewhere,
someplace like the forest
where moss greets the eye.

I sit under a tree,
my body curved to its trunk,
and I lay out the flowers.

Each one heavy in my hand.
Each one placed lightly onto
the receptive earth.

Music and Torment
to my Mother

I waited all night
staring at prints
of her small feet in the snow.

"They will bring her back,"
I told myself.
She won't leave me alone
in Grandmother's house.
How I longed
to clutch her arm,
to hide in the long black hair,
to hear her voice
say *Zosienko*
in a tone more moving
than Chopin.

I climbed the curved stairs
to Grandma's home.
The walls silent.
A hole in the bed
she slept in.
I rolled in the sheets
in search of her scent,
held in my hands
the golden "die-nots"
she used to gather.

Worrying Grandma or Aunt Fela
with her long fingernails
might hear me,
I cried myself to sleep.

Mother, in a Scarlatti smile,
held her arms out to me
when a sharp blade
cut off her hands.

I woke up in the dark room.,
Grandma snoring
in the bed next to me.

"What happened
to my Mother's arms?" I asked.

Trolls came to my bed,
The skin loose on their hands,
primordial lizards,
heads with three or four eyes
staring into my face.
The room full of dreadful arms
and among them
the delicate arms of my Mother.
They wouldn't let her
close to me.
"Mamusiu," I screamed.
Grandma turned,
raised her head,
then snored again.

I looked in the window
gazed at the door.
"When will my Mother
come back?"
my heart asked.
She will protect me
from the soldiers, the hangmen,
at bedtime she will read again
a marvelous fairy tale,
a poem rhyming – music.

A frail dawn
seeped through the window.
The gray sky drizzled.
Small drops drummed on the glass.
How sad and forlorn
was the world outside.

Grandma's home was silent.
No one knocked on the door,
nor did anyone walk outside
wearing a long seal coat.

And then came the noise
of hunger.
The sound of starving tongues roared.
Everyone thought about food,
dreamed of bread,
imagined a piece of horse meat
served on a plate.

I waited for my mother,
my nose cold against
the glass window
calling her name only at night
when no one could hear me,
wearing the one polka-dot dress
she left me.

I waited like the chair
no one came to sit on,
the pot no one cooked soup in,
the oak tree
no child sat under.

Today, the shawl of her hair remains
to wrap me at night.

In the Arms of War

Grandmother in 1941

She lost the flesh
of her body,
her face slimmer
the eyes sadder.

Her head bent
over potato peels
she washed
for our supper.

She still wore a kerchief
to hide her hair
as in the days
she walked
with grandfather to shul

wearing a long satin dress
over her wide body
the small purse
with a pearl clasp in her hand.

Later she sat in the kitchen
weeping, uttering the same sentences

over and over again,

"the oldest and the youngest,
the youngest and the oldest
          gone."

Water in the sink
mixed with tears
as her worn hands
over and over washing.

At the Table

Darning socks,
a silver thimble
on her right forefinger

keeps her from thinking
about what is happening
to her people
in those cold barracks
and forgotten fields,
forced to line up
for slaughter.

She sits with the basket
full of socks
each with a hole
that demands her attention.
She would rather suffer
than inflict suffering, she thinks.

In this tiny room
they use the bed for a table
covered with a torn embroidered cloth
they had managed to keep.

Each time she finishes
mending a hole
she pulls the thread twice
making a knot
then biting it off
with her even teeth.

He turns a page in his book
though he can't remember
a single word,
the letters blurred
like the sky outside
their window.

Der Meister

A slight man you were
with your freckled face
and brown cap.
You supervised our work
at the aviation factory,
we marched to each dawn
from Ravensbruck
concentration camp.

Beneath the table
where I worked
you let me wash
the only undergarment
I possessed,
warming the water
with a torch.

When the "Boots" came near
you tapped me lightly
with your foot
and I jumped up
to my place
at the table.

You brought tidbits
of cookie,
the forbidden chocolate candy,
a piece of banana.
I ate them in the bathroom
praying no one would find me.

You told me
The Gestapo would kill us all
before the war's end.
Herr Meister,
you promised to hide me
in your cellar.

One day you disappeared
and in your place stood
a hard-mouthed man
who didn't talk to me.

I worried, Herr Meister
you might have been punished
for your kindness.
For decades I looked
for your freckled face
and small hands
with that wart on your forefinger.

Marysin

We ran secretly
Josh and I.

Through
the ghetto's
barbed wire

from small rooms
kitchens empty
of food

we ran silently
like thieves
to the one place
that welcomed us.

The sun shined there.
The grass was still green.
Even the flowers
dared to bloom.

We sat hand in hand
and whispered
so the trees would not hear us,
so the birds would not see us,

but maybe God would awaken
from his stupor.

In the Ghetto

In a tiny room
I teach my little sister
the letters of her name.
She is tiny, too.
Doesn't grow much
on water and bread.
Her cheeks sunk
and the small body skinny.
She doesn't jump like a child.
No place to leap or hop.
She doesn't laugh.
No funny jokes told in this room.

Old skirts hang on her bones,
a scarecrow.

Lice multiply in our hair.
Grandmother kills the lice
with her fingernails
click, click. New eggs cling.

My little sister hardly speaks,
her tongue has grown large
in her throat. She waits
for a crumb of bread,
a kind word from our father.
And her eyes are like our father's.
A sad gray.
She cannot cry. There is no one listening.
Everyone is done in by the horror.

She learns
the letters of her name,
MIRIAM... In a tiny room
she learns to spell it
preparing for the day
she will take it with her
into a different world...

The Rosh Hashana Card

September days shrink
into darkness
the yellow russet leaves falling.

I think of you
welcoming *Shana Hachadasha*,
saying the blessings
in *Ashkenazi* tongue,

your hands trembling
over the food,
lips whispering —
"May we all be here next year."

You didn't make it, Father.
I hold in my hands
the blank Rosh Hashana card.

In Ravensbruck

"Two Winds" by Julian Tuwim

Perhaps there were leaves rustling in a field.
I couldn't see
through the windows covered with soot.
Maybe a wind blew in the meadow,
though I didn't hear it.

Inside the barrack,
(an anxious rectangle)
three sips of water in a tin can,
five crumbs of blind bread.
A sack full of straw — a bed.
The flimsy gray jacket
full of lice — a blanket.

"One wind in the meadow blew."
There must have been a sky somewhere,
children going to school,
drinking milk in the morning.
In this anxious rectangle
two sips of water in a tin can,
three crumbs of blind bread.

Words tumbled in my head,
at night when nothing stirred,
Words, heavy at first
from a forgotten well.
"One wind in the meadow blew.
A second wind in the garden flew.
The leaves chased and embraced
Second Wind."

The Line

We stood
in a long
line
moving slowly.

A crooked
line
bulging
from inside
and outside.

Skin
on our faces
white tissue
bodies
bones
without
marrow

upon feet
dragging
in
oversized
shoes
hardly
stirring
the dust.

In a line
moving
slowly
we stood still.

Words like Pomegranates

This instrument
so small
to ignite miles of words.
Whole trails
of weird curling trees
such crazy heavens.

Fruit doesn't always ripen
in this paradise.
Apples hang among
the leaves
like a prayer
for rosy cheeks.
Snakes hibernate for seasons
without end,
forgetting to shed their skin.

Nothing is predictable here,
like your toothbrush
in the morning,
or the milk
delivered to your door.

Here,
the houses survive,
the chimneys
with their smoke
feed the earth.

The Pail of Shit

In a dark bunker
we passed
a pail of shit

from one hand
to another
the urine reeked

we stood cold
starved
bodies thin wafers

skin transparent
on our faces
as if we were
about to enter
the world of heaven
or hell

in striped uniforms
we stood

the pail of shit
passed from
one trembling hand
to another

we didn't see
food for days
yet our bodies
continued to eliminate
and eliminate

we looked through each other
like ghosts

held on to the pail of shit
that linked us.

The Treasure

Every day, I ate the middle
of each slice of bread,
and removed the crust
to be saved
for another day.
I placed these delicate rations
in a yellow sack.

I wanted to devour them,
one crust at a time,
but saved them instead
chanting —

"I won't be hungry
I'll have my treasure."

During an air-raid,
forced out on the snow
I left the bread behind.
Cold air stabbed at my nose
as we walked to the bunker,
as we lowered ourselves
into the dark,
waiting for the bombs
to stop falling.

Back in the barrack,
the empty yellow sack
dangled on the bunk
as if the wind
had blown inside it.
The crusts of bread were gone.
Even the crumbs, nowhere
to be found.

They stole my bread...
the other prisoners
eating the scraps
of my existence.

I didn't ask,
didn't inquire
of the starved faces around me.

I just ate the crusts
one piece at a time,
a treasure to be consumed.
Nothing to be saved.

Germany 1945

So many partings after the war...

The young Russian soldier
talked for hours
about his motherland
how happy he would be
to return home,
how lucky he was to survive
while his comrades
perished in the war.

"We are both survivors,"
I thought.

He told me
about twenty-six watches
buried in his backyard.
"Come with me to Russia
and be my wife," he said.
I was fourteen.

Twenty-six watches,
a strange concept of "wealth," I thought,
unfamiliar as I was
with the Russian condition.

Tilting my head,
I politely declined.

Sitting by the window
I heard the soldiers marching
and knew he was gone,
off to the motherland
off to the treasure
he'd so wisely buried.

On the Way Back to Poland, 1945

Sitting in the living room
of the German house
after supper,
Tzima, Halina,
Rachelka and I
discussed plans
for the future.
What will we do
with all this freedom?
Run in the street?
Taste the sun?
Chase the wind
go to the store
to smell fat sausages
and cheeses?

Suddenly a Russian soldier
stood in the door.
He staggered into the room,
looked around
with blood-shot eyes.
The women slipped out
and I alone remained
with the drunken soldier.
Now that I was free again,
I refused to run and hide.

The soldier drew a revolver
and followed me.
I confronted him.
Retreating slowly,
we made several rounds
about the table,
and he stopped.
Something was troubling him.
The revolver dropped
from his hand,
and he started crying.
He reached into his shirt
and drew out a small,
tarnished star of David.

"I am a Jew, " he said.
"The war makes beasts of us."
I stared at him.
I had little sympathy

for the Jewish soldier.
How dare he come and accost us
after Auschwitz and Treblinka.

"Get out," I said.
"You don't belong here."
He put his revolver back
and staggered to the door.
"I am not a beast," he repeated.

I closed the door
behind him.
After Auschwitz,
after Treblinka,
who among us, can say
we are not animals,
we are not beasts.

Tzima, Halina, and Rachelka
crept back into the room.
"Is he gone?" they asked.
"Yes," I said. "He is gone."
Then we drank our tea,
and went back to talking
about the future,
all the freedom
that lay before us.

Faces

Where is the man I love
who carries flowers
to my door?
Who walks so fast
I can't catch him,
the man who takes me
underground
deep in the heart of the city,
where the earth is wet
and only a small light
shines my way?
All the faces
all the dark eyes
all the dead-end alleys,
unable to find
the man I love...

The man I love
carries flowers to my door,
his curly head bowed
in the desert sun.

He turns quickly,
walks fast,
flowers in
his hand.

I see the back
of his black
coat,

follow him
through
narrow streets,
dark alleys,

walk the city,
the railroad tracks
under bridges
where beggars settle in
for the night.

I look at faces
surrounded
by black curls,

I follow every black coat
every slim silhouette
every curly head of hair
fading in the desert sun.

Neitzana

*"She ran out from the sun and no one
dared to protect her." — a dream*

She ran out from the sun
and shadows danced on her body,
her hair sprinkled with gold threads
her eyes and step light
as a bird's foot.
Her breasts, honey combs.
On her fingers, amber rings.
a sash of yellow leaves circled her waist
and she held a bouquet of yellow roses
in her hand.

The face of the sky
spit rain from a purple mouth.
She ran out from the sun
from yellow whispers of love

and Neitzana was struck.
The yellow roses swam in puddles,
strewn petals carried by a stream.
Her body lost the shadows of the sun.
Her dress was plain.
Water washed the honey
from her breasts.

She still had the amber rings
and the sash of yellow leaves
around her waist

as she staggered to a tree
and rested against its trunk,
waiting for the sky
to regain its composure.

And I thought:
How do such creatures exist?
There is no one to protect them
when the sky turns grim.

Kol Nidre, 1985

The chanting haunts me,
the low weeping sound,

as children crawl
over the knees of their parents
and the holy books.

Men in solemn suits
women in their best dresses

gathered
on the day of judgement.

I sit alone,
he who was with me
since my inception is gone.

In the empty chair to my right
I see his shriveled hands
on the sidur.

They are like mine
folded now in my lap.

Miriam

I hold your Tanach
in my hand
in the carefully embroidered
linen cover
yellowed over time.

Inside, your name
inscribed
in small letters —
"Miriam."

Each year
on Simchat Torah
I take your Tanach
to Jewish children.

I tell them
about the young girl
in Huldah
dressed in blue and white.

A young girl with golden hair
who learned to laugh in freedom
learned to eat and to study.

I hold your Tanach, Miriam
and raise my fist
to heaven.

Yom Kippur

The morning without color.
The sky white
like the cloth on Yom Kippur.
As if all could be erased,
all the blemishes black and red
the passing year painted.

As if I could bring this morning
a blank canvas
to God and to myself.
All could be written
in new letters
new colors,
like the rain
that fell yesterday.

I bring to the new year,
to the day of atonement
a black heart.

What else can be said to God today?
a whisper, a cry,
a silent prayer?

It is time for God to speak.

Erev Rosh Hashana

Aseh Imanu Zedakah Vahesed.
And I think yes. I could use
a little Zedakah, a drop of Hesed.
One sliver
of an apple dipped in honey.

I know little about the Book of Life.
The angel of death held me in his grip
for a long time as the seasons multiplied.

There must be a third book
for those who do not die from disease
or an accident on the freeway.
They flap instead with the wings
of Malach Hamavet,
their breath emanating from the body
in a chaotic rhythm.

A soul flutters in turmoil
a tree succumbs to the earth
but its leaves still move.

So why not fly on black wings
to a place that could be
gehenom
skeletons and skulls
in a great pile.
Bones of those perished.

Yet the heart perseveres,
pumping blood.
The blood of those
gone before us Al Kidush Hashem.
We who have not turned
to skeletons,
our skulls still covered with flesh,
eyes with a glimmer of hope.

The War

Don't recite poems
to me about Auschwitz
and Ravensbruck.
The chimneys burned my hair
and cut my arms.

Don't tell me
how many Jews
were killed in Poland.

I don't want to hear
that your little daughter
died in flames.
All my daughters
with innocent eyes
died in the famous chambers.

Talking about it— you think
it's the same
as eating a banana.

Just sit with me quietly
in the dark
and let the trees speak.

From the Land of Israel

For Amos in Huldah

The girls dipped slim fingers
into the ringlets of your black hair.
With their prettiest smiles
they shimmied their hips against you.
Blinking your eyes like black cherries,
you laughed and laughed.
A true native of the land
of milk and cactus.

At night Palmach crowded the kitchen.
Young men and women in green uniforms,
stens on their shoulders.
To the battle of Latrun, Latrun
on the way to Jerusalem. Baderech Le Yirushalayim.
Israel born two days since. Our ears glued
to the old fashioned boxes, we counted the U.N. Votes.
We stormed the dining hall
and danced the horah till dawn.

I walked with you that night,
the moon round and complete.
Your laughter tingled in the battle air.
Your arm warm at my waist
I slipped a hand into the pocket of your green coat,
and touched the sten on your shoulder.
To Latrun on the way to Jerusalem,
Baderech Le Yirushalayim.
I remembered the vow:
"If I forget you Jerusalem,
my right hand will wither."
"Yim Eshkachech Yirushalayim, Yimani Tekamesh."

The boys returned from Latrun,
carried on stretchers, wrapped in shrouds.
I looked for you, for your black hair,
for the ringlets on your forehead.

You did not return. Not even in a shroud.
The jaws of Latrun swallowed you.
On the way to Jerusalem.
Baderech Le Yirushalayim.

Esty

Her enormous
eyes
magnetize.

Waters
you haven't
seen before.

Blue waters,
the azure waters
of summer.

Eyes you
cannot leave.
Eyes
that always speak.
Quiet
on a summer night.

Angry,
darts flying.

Sad,
drowning in gray.

Her splendid eyes
a well
in which one
could drown or be saved.

Wheels for Ron

Remember your first bicycle?
The orange bike on two wheels
we bought used for six dollars.
You rode it with the determination
of a bull, falling,
scraping your knees.
And you were only four.

You have been on wheels ever since.
The motorcycles you raced
as my heart sped
seeing you turn the corner
at the speed of light.

I like your cars better.
Beautiful masterpieces
shining inside out.

Now, you are on two wheels again,
a sophisticated mountain bike
doing somersaults
under your precise direction.
You take a bunch of novices with you
and soon they spill onto the trail
losing wheels and balance.

You too scrape your knees
riding a dangerous hill.
But you are sturdy today.
Your hands not always
on the steering wheel.

You produce admirable pages of work.
Your mind ticks
like a new clock.

Are you, like the living world in March,
preparing for a new cycle?

For Esty on May Thirty First

On the day you turn twenty-five
your eyes of an undefined color
will change from blue to gray to green
as they so often do.
Your hair will shine red
each time the sun finds it.

Dreams of love
and fantasies of splendor
so fresh in your thoughts
and the potency is plentiful.

I will love you on this day
as on every other day,
simply and imperfectly,
remembering the tiny girl
in my arms,
her eyes so large in her face.

But today you have fallen
into your own arms
and are walking
on your own royal highway.

In a Fairfax Bakery

Golden challahs
cover the the shelves
along with
assorted bagels.

Poppy seed cake
strudel and honey cake
displayed behind glass

a woman stands
behind the counter
her face white
as the dress she wears

the skin so thin
a smile on her
kind face

she works fast
slices the bread
collects the money
runs to the baker
for missing items

on her arm
above the wrist
branded in blue

I notice
the numbers.

My heart races,
I want to embrace her
but I don't.
I leave the bakery
with my challah in hand,
my anguished heart.

Survivor

"I feel guilty being alive"
I often hear Jews say
to someone who survived.
Survived? Once you have been there
you never really leave.
You survived death,
but there is another death
that follows you.

I live with images.
A woman on a stretcher
struck on liberation day.
We ran for freedom
as bullets whistled
over charred bodies
of German soldiers,
swastikas burning in the rubble.

The dead woman haunts me.
Why did she die on that day,
when the air was pungent
with a new spring and, a new freedom?

The swastikas turned to ashes
on that April day.
I thought the world
was coming back to life.

But no! We starve
ourselves to death
and look at the numbers
etched on our arms.

We come back
to the world of living,
to those who can't bear
to look in our eyes.

Eternity In One Man
For Lenny

There was this shock
of white hair
that preceded him
wherever he went.
As if a light
walked with him
throughout his life.

The smile, yes,
that unmistakable smile,
all goodness and sapphires.

Lenny's work on this earth,
like Mount Nevo
and the river Jordan
was immeasurable.
All accented
with politeness and good will.

The Goss clan. Sons and
a daughter, grandchildren,
Hilda's sister.
As close to one another
as strawberries in a field.
Each carries a part
of Lenny inside.

The entire congregation
embraces Hilda
and thus keeps Lenny alive.
The compassion
flows to her
in a steady stream.

And Lenny would have
felt proud
if he could view it
from above,
if he could see
that what he seeded
still blooms.

Back to the Earth
For Yitzhak

Yitzhak, Yitzhak,
voices rise all around him
as he appears in his famous kippah,
his eyes glistening like olives,
he's subdued today.

So you wouldn't think
this slight man
could fill the hall
with exuberance and joy.
Everyone wants to kiss him,
to brush his sleeve,

yet he almost reached the gates of heaven once,
when God called on him: "Yitzhak,"
and he answered: "Heneni."
And Elohim said to him:

"Return to earth and teach,
your work is weighed in diamonds."

The adults,
their brains itching,
wait for him there.

And the children, the children
wait too with hungry eyes.

Voices

Nearing a crow,
the bird takes off
with a bewildering sound.
It's afraid of me
and I am afraid of the shrieking.

Other sounds come to mind.
The stormy voice of my father
thundering voices of the Gestapo.

Today I enjoy
voices soft like suds
the white beard of my grandfather
I remember
the song of the lark at dawn
the melodious voice
of my granddaughter.

And the ever powerful
sound of the Shma.

Tragic Irony

I used to think
every man got an erection
the moment he laid eyes on me.
Time refuted erotica
and I discovered my real talents.

A poetic body with a mouth that speaks
in seasoned verse,
articulates new lines and stanzas,
kisses of the muse and to the muse.

My eyes are bold, not seductive.
My arms, the most eloquent of birds
embrace ever-new trees.
My toes write question marks
in the sand.

Men listen and gaze at me.
They think, I think,
that I am not a body at twilight
but have a clarity that baffles.

A Sparrow

As I approach
the bird opens his tiny beak,
opens his wings
and flies into the sky.

My steps – does the sidewalk tremble?
my giant feet
must frighten the creature
at home in the wind
living on crumbs, on drops of water.

And I tremble too.
My history of terror,
a dread that remains.
A burglar might force
the door open.
In the dark I see violent faces.

But we both somehow survive,
the sparrow and I.
One longing to fly away from the earth
the other at home in the wind.

With my Cousin

Words pour like amber
from his mouth
and seep into my heart.
Long words, short words,
whole sentences uttered in anguish,
the history of his life,
without periods or commas,
words that envelop me.

His blue faded eyes
glisten at times
as the words flow
without restraint,
interrupted only by two apricots
we consume together,
interrupted only by the doctor
who comes to tell us
his wife is out of surgery.

And still I listen until dusk
when we both fall silent
over salmon and wine.

Dan Nacht

The lover from my days
in Tel-Aviv,
an attorney who rode a vespa.
The large toe of his foot
was missing, cut off
in the 48 war.
"Don't worry," he said with a wink
"I am still whole
despite the missing toe."

Dan emerges out of cobwebs
still charming and erudite.
The cactus prickled his hand once.
He asks to marry me
and I agree immediately,
fearing he will get lost again
in Euripides.

We loved, and it was good,
as God said, when on the fifth day
he created flying creatures
and commanded them to multiply.

I tried on a sun flower hat and Dan said
"You shine like a hundred emeralds"
Then I took off the hat, and turned to him.
"And now?" I asked.

"Tamid Yafa," he whispered. "You are beautiful always."

And so were my days in Tel-Aviv
full of light and cactus.

Ilan Ramon

You vanished
from the heavenly skies
like fog
giving space to the sun,
and the astro you loved so much.
Stars and moon,
you could see them glorious
from the shuttle you lived in
for sixteen days
with your astronaut friends.

You took with you
the experiments of school children,
one about the movements of ants,
hopeful
they would return with you,
You took a Torah and a drawing
entitled Moon Landscape
done by fourteen year old Peter Ginz,
a prisoner at Terezin
who died later in Auschwitz,

thus conveying your intent.
You set out to realize
the boy's dream,
and to honor a piece of history
since your mother
was a Shoa survivor.

You didn't undertake
this mission for yourself, you said,
but for others.

I watched you
march to the shuttle
in your orange space suit,
a gleam in your eye, your step firm.

I waited to see you again
but the heavenly skies claimed you.
I will not have the mitzvah

to attend your funeral. Eretz Israel
will take your remains, and you will rest
in the land
you loved so dearly.

An Evening Full of Roses

Where is my home?
The floor, a pillow,
a tree that talks in the wind.
A little fairy hut
with a sweet bench
made from the birch
of my childhood.

Where is my home?
In that stark desert
with its merciless sun?
Wars never sleep,
nor do those they leave behind.
And love hasn't gone to sleep either.
The evenings are still full of roses.
God has another name.

Masada

The old fortress
in its grandeur of ruins.
I walk with ease

as if my feet belong here.
I remember the stones,
the small ones I roll beneath my toes,
the large ones I sit on,
and the ones I embrace with both my arms.

Eilat in January, 1991

The sun is hot in a flawless sky,
the water calm and blue
like my mother's apron.

The tourists have taken
their cameras elsewhere.
In the luxurious hotels
the porters are on holiday.

Waiters approach us in the streets.
They offer a meat dinner for half price.
The hungry cab drivers stop us.

I watch a cat limp on one leg
and wonder
in which war was he injured.

The Warbler

The little bird
sat in the corner of my yard,
and I wondered why it waited there
so quietly and didn't fly
like the other chicadees on the tree
that chattered and flapped their wings.
It let me come close
and I talked to the bird
with gray feathers,
its eyes moving from side to side
like bouncing beans.

How come you sit here like a hen?
A cat could come and snatch you.
My wing is hurt, the bird warbled,
I cannot fly.

But you must, I said.
You must fly,
or the cat will come
and pluck you.

The bird moved its tail
with great effort,
and echoed: I must try to fly
I must try to fly
or the cat will come and snatch me.
It spread the one wing
and folded it.

... I touched the bird
and it moved from my finger like a spark,
wings flapping in the sky—
a gray cloud.

Voices from an Old House

In the house
a torn blanket covers
the Terra Cotta women
on biting winter nights.
They alone remain in the house,
growing Modigliani necks,
stretching their heads to see
the world they define.
But no one comes
and no sound is heard.

No steam rises from pots
in the kitchen.
In the sink, no hands scrub the dishes clean.
No hand lifts them
from this place of waiting.
If they could
they would wail
long into the vacant night.

Terra Cotta Women

"The only woman awake
is the woman
who heard the flute
at 4:00 in the morning."
                    Kabir

In the night I awake,
choking on my own breath,
black all around me,
the leaves outside the window
quiet and watchful.

The phone rings at that hour
when birds sleep
and bats open
their sinister wings.

I stumble over a chair.
Not a disaster I pray.
Not a reason
for my daughter or son
to cry over the phone.

I find my voice
close to the cold receiver.
It doesn't sound like bells
or a flute
but it does utter a hello.

At the other end, silence.
Why don't they whisper or cry?
Yell an obscenity,
anything but silence.

I look around the room.
The "WOMEN in Clay,"
miniature sculptures
full of pain and longing.
Their long hair whispers.
Secrets. Or else they're
calling to someone
on the dead telephone.

They sit on the mantle,
on tables. Their tongues
twisted. Lips sealed
with black ink.

A crowd of women. A congregation.
They could assemble in the street,
They could dance in the alley,
in the courtyard.
Their long hair would sweep
the air clean.

When their twisted tongues unfold,
words dribble off
like pennies from
a torn pocket.

Not a blessed rain
their words
not a shower of eloquence,
but beads in a necklace
newly strung.

A Kugel

A kugel, a kigel
a Jewish fish dish.
You can make a kugel
from any old bugel.
You just take a bigel
and you make a kigel.
You mix the fish, swish,
you add the eggs plimp plimp.

You take potatoes
broccoli or tomatoes,
and add onions
raisins and poponions.
Mix it all around with a spoon,
and slide it into the oven
like a good kugel deserves.
To heat, to expand.
To become plump and soft inside,
firm on the outer side.
To become a kugel
for your very special table of Shabbat.

Grandmother's House in Poland

The freshly polished silver
in grandmother's house

the white linen table-cloth
smells of sun and wind,
the forks blink
to the spoons.

We gathered
around the oak table,
ate red beet borscht
and mashed potatoes,
the bread fresh from the oven.

Pretty aunt Balbina
in long laced
ballet shoes.

Aunt Fela
who scratched my face
with her long fingernails.

My mother
with the black crown of hair.

Uncle Yulek,
loved to smile.
He rode motorcycles.

And my uncle Yumek
had me recite poems
for his friends.

Uncle Moniek's eyes
were shining chestnuts
in the fall.

Tall grandfather Mordkowicz
loved to smoke
cigarettes at night
as the rest of us slept,
or pretended to.

My ample grandmother
ruled the house
with an iron baton.
I slept in a special room,
waiting for my mother to come
kiss me good night
and recite a Polish poem.

2

Yellow stars appeared
in the Polish skies
as the trains rolled
to Auschwitz.

My family, too.
Though there are no graves.
Their bones
mingled with other bones
disintegrated by now.
No one knows where.

And if I knew
how could I tell their bones
from other bones?
How could I find
the black crown of
my mother's hair?

They are all before me
the saints and the apparitions
when I recite Kaddish
each Shabbat morning.

In Grandmother's house,
I played and dreamed.

Beneath the table
with its white tablecloth
smelling of sun and wind,

the forks blinked to the spoons.

A Jolting Surprise

How exuberant one must be,
to cry out loud,
to stand in awe, silent

rather than running home
through the thin flakes of snow
falling like rain
from a purple heaven.
There, the eyes are bewildered
by what they see:
three rainbows at once!

The vivid stripes
shaped like a bow,
one wants them to exist forever,
beyond one's own time.
The world beneath it
is a sea of shells glittering
in the sun.

The covenant with Noah
to keep floods from the earth
will not be forgotten.

Poppies

In the evening,
the last rays of sun
on a wall of this room
on the carpet expanded
before shrinking again
to their usual size,
the sun so generous
to give a glimpse of the divine
before its departure
into night.

The poppies too fold
their golden petals
like the day folding up
its belongings.

Now they are little flutes
for the fingers,
little orange scrolls that remain
when the sun disappears
into night.

Loss

For Lorraine

Gnaws at the heart,
at the brain,
your thoughts scattered
like a deck of cards.
The queen cannot find the king
so she weeps.

You have lost some essential
part of yourself
as if the tears washed it away.
There are moments
when you don't want to be strong,
you don't want to smile
to everyone around you
as if the world still existed.

And then one morning you hear a lark

warble by your window.
A pink blossom smiles,
knowing it is beautiful.
Another day has come,
full of hope and promise.
Life is calling on you.

Skylight

On the skylight
window pane
the frost.
White flowers
that grew in the night
now drip
down the glass
losing their cold shapes
in the sun.

What's in a Name

I'd like to ask my father
Why I was named Zofia,
the heroine
of Adam Mickiewicz's classic
Pan Tadeusz,
but he is between clouds, musing.
There is only the unearthly beat
of his heart.

I'd like to ask my mother
Why I was given such a name
before she gave her last breath
to the Nazis when I was
still a child.

I'd like to ask my uncles
why I was named Zofia
but they too went
to their respective kingdoms
The walls may scream, but they won't talk.

Only the white marguerites
in a vase
nod their graceful heads,
repeat my name as a blessing
and a curse:
Zofia, Zofia, Zofia.

Starla

How much I love her.
The little girl
with the large blue eyes
and skin
fair as cream.
I would go anywhere
with her.
Climb a mountain
sit on a rock,
rock her in my arms.

I hear her murmur
her first words—
hot, horse, puppy,
orange, bear
in a voice as sweet
as glass bells.

I help her climb
tall steps
holding her tiny hand.
We make sounds together
and she touches my face
with her little nose.
We walk.
I follow her and watch.
Is there something
in her mouth
that's not supposed to be,
is she holding
a dangerous object?

Together,
we make a team.
One who has gone
through the trials of life,
and the other
just beginning
on a starlit path.

Skyler

He is quite a trooper
at age three he rides
a bicycle on two wheels.
Rides a scooter
up and down the hill
with perfect balance.
He loves to be on wheels
whether two or four.

He fusses at times
but returns in a jiffy
to his gorgeous self.
Eyes, black cherries smiling.

Skyler has small shaped
hands and feet. But oh,
do they know how to work.
He helps the men working
on the driveway of his home,
he treats them with blue
and purple popsicles.

The Sweetest One

How much I love her,
the girl with enormous eyes.
Lapis light.
Skin fair as cream.
Lips a fresh tulip.

She makes spinach
out of green felt,
grinding it in a wooden contraption.

She creates a snow storm
in the living room
with baby powder.

She slips her small hand
into my old one
and we go cruising the town.

We find a skeleton of a large bird,
the bones like a puzzle,
impeccably clean.

Starla hides behind me
and cries out like a peacock,
"Beas, you are dead when you
are a skeleton?"

When it's time to leave
she throws her arms around me.
"Beas, can you sleep in my house?," she says.

A New Coat

To write from despair
was easier.
Words slid in tears
and fell onto the page.

Words dipped in maror, horse-radish.
Words fell like potatoes from a sack,
dark spuds that tore the page
with their unbearable weight.

Now there isn't enough sweetness
to fill the page.

I grope each morning
for a sound, a feeling, a phrase,
unaccustomed to living
without misery.

A black coat has been
taken from my shoulders,
and I'm left shivering in sunshine,
waiting for a new weave.

A Happiness

Years of darkness,
of father's dark suit,
of mother's seal coat
of the old grandfather clock
behind which
I was forbidden to play.

Then today,
the raven on the window sill
flies off
and does not return.
Suddenly,
the house rings,
a voice singing.

Today, my home rings
a voice singing,
a lost daughter returns home.

Crawled out from behind
the grandfather clock,
she plays with her sleepy doll,
blows bubbles in the air
with a blue straw.

A voice can be heard
in this house at dawn
before the sun is visible
with its trail of pink clouds
before the light comes
to the window.

A serene voice from above,
fills every crevice in the house
with music.

The child laughs
the woman smiles
in her mournful dress,
and the poet's voice crackles
from under her bones
like a flame rising up
from the logs
in the fireplace.

www.ingramcontent.com/pod-product-compliance
Lightning Source LLC
LaVergne TN
LVHW091204080426
835509LV00006B/832

* 9 7 8 0 9 4 1 0 1 7 1 3 8 *